Animal Adaptations

By Leigh McClure

Published in 2025 by Cavendish Square Publishing, LLC
2544 Clinton Street Buffalo, NY 14224

Copyright © 2025 by Cavendish Square Publishing, LLC

First Edition

No part of this publication may be reproduced, stored in a retrieval system, or transmitted in any form or by any means—electronic, mechanical, photocopying, recording, or otherwise—without the prior permission of the copyright owner. Request for permission should be addressed to Permissions, Cavendish Square Publishing, 2544 Clinton Street Buffalo, NY 14224. Tel (877) 980-4450; fax (877) 980-4454.

Website: cavendishsq.com

This publication represents the opinions and views of the author based on their personal experience, knowledge, and research. The information in this book serves as a general guide only. The author and publisher have used their best efforts in preparing this book and disclaim liability rising directly or indirectly from the use and application of this book.

All websites were available and accurate when this book was sent to press.

Library of Congress Cataloging-in-Publication Data

Names: McClure, Leigh, author.
Title: Animal adaptations / Leigh McClure.
Description: Buffalo, NY : Cavendish Square Publishing, [2025] | Series: The inside guide: biology basics | Includes bibliographical references and index.
Identifiers: LCCN 2024033481 (print) | LCCN 2024033482 (ebook) | ISBN 9781502673275 (library binding) | ISBN 9781502673268 (paperback) | ISBN 9781502673282 (ebook)
Classification: LCC QH546 (print) | LCC QH546 (ebook) | DDC 591.47/2–dc23/eng/20240812
LC record available at https://lccn.loc.gov/2024033481
LC ebook record available at https://lccn.loc.gov/2024033482

Editor: Caitie McAneney
Copyeditor: Nicole Horning
Designer: Deanna Lepovich

The photographs in this book are used by permission and through the courtesy of: Cover Henner Damke/Shutterstock.com; p. 4 yunus topal/Shutterstock.com; p. 6 OLGA ALEXANDROVA/Shutterstock.com; p. 7 Jack FotoVerse/Shutterstock.com; p. 8 Foto Mous/Shutterstock.com; p. 9 Mircea Costina/Shutterstock.com; p. 10 Fitawoman/Shutterstock.com; p. 12 GTW/Shutterstock.com; p. 13 Jukka Jantunen/Shutterstock.com; p. 14 LuckyStep/Shutterstock.com; p. 16 James C Farr/Shutterstock.com; p. 18 Mark Doherty/Shutterstock.com; p. 20 frank60/Shutterstock.com; p. 21 Tyler Fox/Shutterstock.com; p. 22 Darwin's finches by Gould/Wikimedia Commons; p. 24 Wirestock Creators/Shutterstock.com; p. 26 MPH Photos/Shutterstock.com; p. 27 Agnieszka Bacal/Shutterstock.com; p. 28 (top) Jan Martin Will/Shutterstock.com; p. 28 (bottom) PARALAXIS/Shutterstock.com; p. 29 (top) Vladimir Turkenich/Shutterstock.com; p. 29 (bottom) Joseph Hendrickson/Shutterstock.com.

Some of the images in this book illustrate individuals who are models. The depictions do not imply actual situations or events.

CPSIA compliance information: Batch #CWCSQ25: For further information contact Cavendish Square Publishing LLC at 1-877-980-4450.

Printed in the United States of America

CONTENTS

Chapter One: 5
   Survival of the Fittest

Chapter Two: 11
   Adapting to the Environment

Chapter Three: 17
   Blending In

Chapter Four: 23
   Let's Find Food!

Think About It!   28

Glossary   30

Find Out More   31

Index   32

Penguins are perfectly adapted to their Arctic environment. They can survive in low temperatures that most other animals couldn't stand.

SURVIVAL OF THE FITTEST

Chapter One

Why do giraffes have long necks? Why are sharks able to smell one drop of blood in the water around them? You may have noticed that animals look and act differently from each other. They all have their special features, skills, and behaviors.

Those differences are often due to adaptations. Adaptations are changes in the body or behavior that help an animal live in their environment, or surroundings. Over many millions of years, animals have adapted to find and eat food, and secure **mates** and shelter. Those animals that have helpful features are the fittest for their environment, and their reward is survival.

Fast Fact
Some animals change their appearance from season to season. Arctic hares are brown during the warmer months, and white in winter months. That's an adaptation.

Why Adapt?

Imagine a penguin dropped in the desert. Do you think it would survive? No! That's because penguins have adapted to cold, wet environments. They have waterproof feathers and the ability to swim for their favorite food—fish.

Animal bodies adapt according to the temperature, availability of water, and

5

White fur helps the Arctic hare blend in with snow in winter.

the food they need in a certain place. For example, camels store fat in their humps so they don't need to eat or drink much while walking across the **barren** desert; the fat is converted, or changed, into energy.

Adaptations also help an animal find prey, escape predators, **attract** a mate, and pass on their **genes** to babies. If an animal can't adapt, they can't survive in a place for very long or have babies.

Predator Adaptations

Animals have adapted to different **terrains** and temperatures. They've also adapted to survive based on where they are in a food chain. Small plant-eating animals are often prey for larger meat-eating animals. These predators use adaptations to find and eat their prey.

The hairy frogfish waits for its prey, then sucks it into its mouth quickly!

Physical adaptations are features on an animal's body that help them survive. Physical adaptations that help predators hunt include sharp teeth, night vision, and strong jaws. For example, saltwater crocodiles have a biting force of 3,700 pounds (1,678.3 kilograms) per square inch!

Predators have also adapted their behavior to help them hunt. For example, some animals, like wolves, hunt in groups. Others, like frogfish, sit and wait for their prey, then sneak-attack them.

Fast Fact

Mountain lions have soft padded paws that help them quietly sneak up on prey.

SCALES AND SHELLS: PANGOLINS AND TURTLES

Some animals have adaptations that protect their bodies from predators' teeth and claws. Shells and hard scales often act as armor. This is most obvious in turtles and tortoises that can quickly pull their head, legs, and arms into their shell whenever they feel a threat, or danger, is coming. Few animals can break through shells with their teeth.

Pangolins are seemingly strange mammals because they are completely covered in scales instead of fur. If the pangolin sees a predator, it curls up into a tight, hard ball, using its scales as armor. Many lizards and crocodiles also use scales as armor.

Pangolins have both prey and predator adaptations. In addition to scaly armor, they have tongues that can be longer than their bodies to eat ants from the ground.

Prey Adaptations

Prey animals need to have adaptations to survive too. Some, such as deer and rabbits, rely on sharp hearing. Their ears are large and can turn in different directions, so they can hear predators approaching.

Some prey animals give warnings if a predator is near. For example, a rattlesnake will make a rattling sound. A beaver will beat its tail against the water. Some will defend themselves. For example, a skunk will spray a stinky oil on anything that gets too close.

Deer have both sharp senses and speed on their side. If they hear a predator, they can quickly run away on long, thin legs.

Fast Fact

A porcupine's adaptation is pretty easy to see—it has sharp points, called quills. These points keep the porcupine from being attacked by predators.

Insulation means the ability to keep heat in. The musk ox's insulation is an adaptation to help it survive in cold weather.

ADAPTING TO THE ENVIRONMENT

Chapter Two

Earth is full of many different kinds of habitats and regions. In the Arctic, it's cold much of the time. Along the equator, it's very hot. High mountains cover some areas, while some places are flat. Some are grassy and full of **vegetation**. Others are sandy and barren.

Animals have adapted to habitats all over the world. Some habitats are extreme, such as the deep sea. Adaptations help animals survive in whatever place they call home.

Animals in the Cold

The Arctic is a habitat with long, cold, dark winters. How can anything survive there? Some animals have a special adaptation—moving from place to place. That's called migration. For example, some birds migrate south in the winter.

Cold-climate mammals often have thick, warm fur. Musk oxen have an undercoat that keeps them warm in freezing-cold temperatures. Underneath a polar bear's skin is a thick layer of fat called blubber that keeps them warm. This insulation is an excellent adaptation!

Fast Fact
The hairs that make up the musk ox's outer coat are very long to protect it from wind and snow.

Polar bears have the thickest fur of any bear on Earth. The top layer is made of clear, hollow tubes that trap air for insulation.

Some animals, such as the grizzly bear, rest through the long, cold winters. Their bodies "shut down" for months to save energy. During this time, their heart rate and breathing slow down.

Desert Creatures

Deserts are also extreme habitats. They are very dry, gaining no more than 10 inches (25.4 centimeters) of rain or snow per year. Many

Mammals such as coyotes shed their winter coats in warm weather.

deserts, such as the Sahara in Africa, are very hot. Temperatures often dip low at night and rise greatly during the day.

Animals have had to adapt to life in deserts. To beat the heat, some animals—like pack rats and Gila monsters—dig holes called burrows. They stay underground for the hottest parts of the day. It's cooler there.

A desert's lack of water is a major challenge. Some animals need very little water to survive, which is an adaptation. For example, kangaroo rats survive eating mostly dry seeds, with no water available.

Fast Fact
Desert animals such as gray foxes are nocturnal, or active at night when it's cooler. Others are more active at dawn and dusk.

Water World

More than 70 percent of Earth is water! Many animals live in bodies of water. Some animals live in the ocean, which is salty. Others live in

BIOLUMINESCENCE

Some ocean creatures have developed an adaptation called bioluminescence. This means they can create their own light. Light is created in a special chemical reaction. It's most noticeable in the deep sea, where everything is very dark.

Female anglerfish have a glowing body part that dangles from their heads like a fishing pole. Curious prey swims closer—then is eaten! Some squids use bioluminescence to scare predators away. They flash their light, then escape. Brittle stars can detach their glowing body parts, so predators go after an arm instead of its owner.

Great white sharks are at the top of the ocean food chain! Their adaptations include their huge size, strong jaws, and many sharp teeth.

Fast Fact

Whales get around in the dark ocean through an adaptation called echolocation. They make a sound, then listen as it bounces off objects.

HABITAT ADAPTATIONS

Desert
- burrowing
- ability to survive with little water
- nocturnal

Arctic
- camouflage, or blend in, with snow in winter
- thick fur or blubber to survive low temperatures

Forest
- ability to climb trees
- prehensile (grasping) tails
- camouflage with leaves and branches

Ocean
- gills or blowholes to take in oxygen
- echolocation
- fins to swim

These are some adaptations that animals may have in each kind of habitat.

bodies of fresh water, such as lakes and ponds. Animals live in marshes and other wetlands too.

Animals that live in water have their own special adaptations. For example, fish use gills to get oxygen under water. Animals need this gas to live. Some ocean animals crawl along the ocean floor using legs. Others swim through the open ocean with fins and special tails.

Marine mammals include dolphins and humpback whales. They breathe and get oxygen through a blowhole on their back, then stay underwater for long periods of time.

This snow leopard blends in with its rocky, snowy surroundings, allowing it to sneak up on prey.

BLENDING IN

Chapter Three

Have you ever seen a bug blend in with tree bark? Have you ever almost stepped on a toad because it was the same color as the mud around it? If so, you've seen camouflage in the wild! Camouflage, or blending in, is an adaptation that's used by prey and predators alike.

Camouflage helps animals hide within their surroundings. This can be helpful for predators when they **stalk** their prey. It can also be useful for prey who want to go unnoticed by predators.

Changing Colors

Some animals have skin, scales, or fur that match the colors of their surroundings. For example, many snakes are the colors of sand, stone, or dirt. Deer blend in with their woody surroundings too.

Other animals change colors to blend in. Some change colors based on the season, appearing brownish in warmer months and white in colder months. Chameleons may change colors

Fast Fact

More than 20 species, or kinds, of animals change from brown to white between summer and winter in the Northern Hemisphere!

17

based on what they're feeling. Octopuses can change both the color and **texture** of their skin to blend in or stand out. A dull color helps the octopus hide in its surroundings. A bright color could warn enemies that the octopus will attack!

Chromatophores are color-changing cells just underneath an octopus's skin that allow it to change color.

SPOTS AND STRIPES

Some animals use patterns on their fur or skin to blend in with their surroundings. Some big cats—such as tigers and leopards—have patterns on their fur that help them blend in with grasses or dull landscapes. "Eyespots" are patterns on butterflies that look like the eyes of owls, which might scare away predators.

Zebra stripes make them stand out against their surroundings—but blend in with each other. They live in large herds. When they all stand together, it's hard for a predator to tell one from the others. This gives each zebra more of a chance of survival.

Super Shapes

Some animals blend in using their special body shape. Bugs are masters of this kind of camouflage! For example, the stick bug looks like a stick with its long, thin body. The orchid mantis looks like an orchid flower. Its brightly-colored body parts appear to be flower petals.

One of the deadliest animals on Earth hides in plain sight. The stonefish looks just like the rocks at the bottom of the seafloor. It has bumpy skin and dull colors. Its mouth is on top of its body, ready to **ambush** its prey. It also has venomous spines, or spikes, that can kill animals or people.

Some stick bugs, also called walking sticks, sway their bodies in the wind to look like a swaying twig.

Fast Fact
The leaf-tailed gecko has a tail that's shaped exactly like a leaf to blend in with the trees it calls home.

Mimicry

Some animals use mimicry to blend in or to trick predators into leaving them alone. To mimic something is to look or act exactly like it. This can be a behavioral or a physical adaptation. The giant swallowtail caterpillar has white and black coloring and a long, thin body that makes it look just like bird poop. It can rest on top of a leaf to fool predators.

Some species of cuckoo birds hide their eggs in the nests of other species. Their eggs may look like the eggs of the other bird. It's a trick. The host bird will raise the cuckoo as its own, feeding the baby cuckoo—even if it's bigger than the host bird.

Fast Fact
Leafy sea dragons mimic sea grasses with their swaying motions.

This isn't bird poop on a leaf. It's a caterpillar!

This journal page shows the different beak shapes that Charles Darwin observed on finches in the Galápagos Islands.

1. Geospiza magnirostris.
3. Geospiza parvula.
2. Geospiza fortis.
4. Certhidea olivasea.

LET'S FIND FOOD!

Chapter Four

Charles Darwin studied small birds called finches on the Galápagos Islands in the 1830s. He noted that finches in different areas had adapted their beak shape based on their food sources. Some had long, pointed beaks for snapping up insects. Others had shorter, wider beaks for cracking seeds.

Eating is a key part of survival. Therefore, many adaptations allow animals to find or eat their food. From super senses to unique body parts, these adaptations help animals live in their environment and remain a part of their food chain.

Fast Fact
Charles Darwin is often called "the father of evolution." Evolution is the process of living things changing over time to fit their environments.

Super Senses

Senses are the ways in which animals experience the world. Senses include sight, hearing, smell, taste, and touch. Many animals have developed sharper senses than those of humans. Some animals have more senses than humans do. For example, sharks can sense the

Snakes use receptors on their tongues to collect chemicals from the air or ground to sense their surroundings.

electrical fields of their prey. That helps them locate prey in the dark ocean.

Butterflies taste through their feet. When they land on a flower, they can tell if it's good to eat from. Bats and whales "see" through echolocation. They use echoes to create a mental image of what's around them.

RAINFOREST ADAPTATIONS

Rainforest animals are perfectly adapted to life in the trees. The flying frog can glide from tree to tree with webbed body parts that act like a parachute. The sloth's colors and slow motion help them blend in with the trees. They've adapted in other ways, too—sloths only have to come down to the ground about once a month to get rid of their waste. Spider monkeys have long, thin arms and a prehensile tail for swinging from branch to branch and grabbing food. Unfortunately, these animals are affected by deforestation, or the cutting down of too many trees. Without their homes, many are finding it hard to survive.

Fast Fact

Prehensile tails can hold or grasp objects. Some species of monkeys and porcupines have prehensile tails.

Reach Up High

Some animals use their body parts to get food that's up high. Giraffes have long necks to reach up into trees for leaves. This adaptation allows them to gather food.

Some animals have adaptations that help them climb up high for food. Sloths and howler monkeys are able to climb up into the top parts of the rainforest. There, they enjoy fruits and leaves that other animals can't reach. Animals that climb for food often have physical adaptations like claws, strong hands, or prehensile tails.

Dig Down Low

Some animals have adapted to life underground. This is where they find their food or make their shelter—or sometimes both. They need special adaptations that help them move in the earth and find their food.

A giraffe's neck can measure up to 6 feet (1.8 meters) long! It allows the giraffe to reach young leaves in trees.

Fast Fact

Earthworms don't have senses of hearing, sight, or smell. Instead, they sense vibrations, or small movements, in the soil around them and sense light through their skin.

Earthworms are unlike any animal in the world. Without arms, legs, eyes, noses, or ears, these creatures have developed adaptations to live underground. They have long, thin bodies that wiggle through the earth. They survive by eating decaying plant and animal matter.

Moles make their homes underground using their special adaptations. They dig tunnels with strong claws shaped like shovels. Underground, they hunt for their favorite food— earthworms!

The star-nosed mole's nose is the most sensitive organ of any animal on Earth. It tells the mole if what they're touching is good to eat.

THINK ABOUT IT!

1. How might warming temperatures affect animals adapted to Arctic environments?

2. How could animals who live in trees be affected by deforestation?

3. Why are predator adaptations important to a food chain?

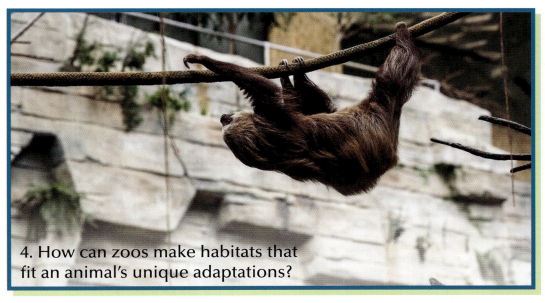

4. How can zoos make habitats that fit an animal's unique adaptations?

GLOSSARY

ambush: To carry out a surprise attack.

attract: To cause someone or something to do or to like something.

barren: With little or no plant growth.

gene: The part of cells that controls the appearance, growth, and other traits of a living thing.

hemisphere: Half of Earth.

mate: One of two animals that come together to produce babies.

receptor: A nerve ending that senses changes in light, temperature, or pressure, and makes the body act in a certain way because of those changes.

sensitive: Able to feel strongly.

stalk: To follow after prey without being noticed.

terrain: A type of land in an area.

texture: The structure, feel, and appearance of something.

vegetation: Plant life in an area.

FIND OUT MORE

Books

Geron, Eric. *Shells*. New York, NY: Children's Press, 2024.

Mikoley, Kate. *20 Fun Facts About Tundra Habitats*. New York, NY: Gareth Stevens Publishing, 2022.

Owen, Ruth. *Animal Camouflage in a Desert*. Minneapolis, MN: Ruby Tuesday Books, 2024.

Websites

Explore Animal Adaptations
naturalhistory.si.edu/education/teaching-resources/life-science/explore-animal-adaptations
Discover how animal adaptations allow certain animals to survive in their environment.

Habitats
kids.nationalgeographic.com/nature/habitats
Explore different habitats around the world and think critically about the adaptations that help animals live there.

Hidden Animals
kids.nationalgeographic.com/wacky-weekend/article/hidden-animals
Check out animal camouflage in the wild with *National Geographic*.

Publisher's note to educators and parents: Our editors have carefully reviewed these websites to ensure that they are suitable for students. Many websites change frequently, however, and we cannot guarantee that a site's future contents will continue to meet our high standards of quality and educational value. Be advised that students should be closely supervised whenever they access the internet.

INDEX

A
Arctic, 5, 11
armor, 8

B
behavior, 5, 7, 20

C
camouflage, 15, 17, 19
claws, 7, 8, 25, 27
cold-climate animals, 11

D
Darwin, Charles, 23
deserts, 5, 6, 12, 13, 15

E
echolocation, 14, 15
evolution, 23

F
food chains, 6, 23

H
habitats, 11, 12, 15

M
mate, 5, 6
mimicry, 20, 21

P
predators, 6, 7, 8, 9, 14, 17, 19, 20
prey, 6, 7, 9, 14, 17, 19, 24

R
rainforest, 25

S
senses, 23, 27
shapes, 19, 20, 23

T
teeth, 7, 8
temperature, 5, 6, 11, 13, 15
threats, 8

U
underground, 13, 26, 27

W
water, 5, 9, 13, 15